VIRGINIA
impressio

photography by Charles Gurche

FARCOUNTRY
PRESS

Right: A moody sun rises over the Atlantic Ocean east of Assateague Island.

Title page: Flowering dogwood on a foggy spring morning.

Front cover: Mabry Mill on the Blue Ridge Parkway.

Back cover: Crabtree Falls in George Washington National Forest.

ISBN 1-56037-193-5
Photographs © 2001 by Charles Gurche
© 2001 Farcountry Press

Created, produced, and designed in the United States.
Printed in Korea

Above: Looking out over the gardens of Stratford Hall, at Stratford, a restored working colonial plantation that dates from the 1730s and was home to four generations of the Lee family; brothers Richard Henry and Francis Lightfoot signed the Declaration of Independence, and future Confederate general Robert E. was born here.

Facing page: Virginia's early English colonists brought the tall yellow-poplar, or tuliptree, to North America.

Woodland Union Church
in Bath County below the
Allegheny Mountains.

Above: Up a relatively easy two-mile trail in Shenandoah County, Big Schloss offers view of Virginia and West Virginia.

Facing page: Sunrise over the Potomac River gilds the portico of Mount Vernon, home to George and Martha Washington.

Sunrise on Lake Prince near Suffolk.

Above: This hunk of granite is balanced atop Old Rag Mountain in Shenandoah National Park.

Facing page: Near Chantilly, Sully Plantation shows visitors life in the first half of the 19th century.

Above: Arlington House was where Robert E. Lee courted his wife, and where they lived from 1831 to 1861; restored to its pre–Civil War appearance, it stands above Arlington National Cemetery.

Facing page: The James River in Bedford County, near where it starts to flow to the sea from the Blue Ridge.

Right: Falling Springs in Alleghany County, a cooling sight on a summer's day.

Facing page: Snow does not stop students on their appointed rounds at University of Virginia, Charlottesville.

Above: The sturdy but simple plantation buildings of Stratford Hall, Stratford.

Facing page: The Blue Ridge Parkway offers 470 miles of scenic driving on the crest of the Blue Ridge Mountains.

Right and above: Arlington National Cemetery honors veterans of United States wars, and includes the Marine Corps memorial that portrays World War II flag-raising on Iwo Jima in the South Pacific.

Above: Autumn vibrancy in southwestern Virginia's Jefferson National Forest.

Facing page: Sunrise magic at Fairy Stone State Park in the southern Blue Ridge.

Above: Coleman Memorial Bridge crosses the York River at Yorktown.

Facing page: Oatlands, near Leesburg, dates from 1804 and exhibits American and French art and antiques collections.

Above: Peaceful evening on the Shenandoah River in Clarke County.

Facing page: The Homestead at Hot Springs, where spas have welcomed guests for generations.

Left: Sugar maples of Jefferson National Forest begin to don autumn finery.

Facing page: The Great Falls of the Potomac River in Fairfax County.

A welcoming carpet of pristine sand
on Assateague Island.

Above: Looking at Fauquier County through Jack Frost's handiwork on Blue Mountain.

Facing page: Longford Lake in Fairfax County gleams with autumn.

Above: St. Thomas Episcopal Church in Abingdon.

Facing page: The Maury River nourishes foothills of the Blue Ridge.

Right: Oxeye daisies and lunaria making a bright springtime statement.

Facing page: Out for an early walk along the Chesapeake Bay.

Above: Wildflowers are only part of the displays at Norfolk Botanical Gardens; azaleas, rhododendrons, and camellias bloom there, too.

Left: Shenandoah National Park's Buck Hollow.

Right: All set for a summer night's storm over Albemarle County.

Facing page: Settled in along the Chesapeake Bay.

It's a long way
down to the town
of Cumberland
Gap, Tennessee,
from Cumberland
Gap National
Historical Park
in Virginia.

Above: At Yorktown, the American colonies won their Revolutionary War, and exhibits today include these cannons brought by French soldiers who fought on the rebels' side.

Left: The Frontier Culture Museum at Staunton explores the homelands left behind by early Virginia colonists, such as this Scots-Irish farm.

Above: Grace Church at Yorktown.

Facing page: Contrasting textures on the Chesapeake Bay.

Frederick County arises coated with ice following a winter storm.

Above: Washington and Lee University, at Lexington, dates from 1749. Its elegant Lee Chapel, built in 1867 by then-president Robert E. Lee, is where he is buried.

Facing page: Loudoun County bursts out with spring.

Above: Historic homes from grand to cozy abound in Williamsburg.

Facing page: Falling Springs Cascades in Alleghany County.

Above: St. Luke's Church, in Isle of Wight County, dates from 1632.

Facing page: Skyline Drive in Shenandoah National Park provides a path through summer's lush landscape.

Arlington
Memorial
Bridge over the
Potomac River.

A touch of autumn haze highlights the brightness of turning leaves, as seen from the Blue Ridge Parkway.

Above: Monticello in Albemarle County was designed by and then housed one of the young nation's finest minds: Thomas Jefferson.

Facing page: Westmoreland State Park's Horsehead Cliffs.

Above: In Abingdon, a 1936 Chevrolet "workhorse" rests for now.

Facing page: Falls of the Little Stony are a refreshing destination in Jefferson National Forest.

Above: Peaks of Otter on the Blue Ridge Parkway is a recreation area of more than 4,000 acres.

Facing page: Assateague Island National Seashore includes 48,000 acres in Virginia and Maryland, between the Atlantic Ocean and Chincoteague Bay.

Above: In the water tupelo forest of Great Dismal Swamp National Wildlife Refuge.

Left: Burkes Garden, also called "God's Thumbprint," is this beautiful bowl of farm fields surrounded by mountains in Tazewell County.

Above: Wattle-and-daub cottages at Jamestown Settlement are like the homes that English colonists built here in 1607.

Right: Sailor's Creek Battlefield Historical Park, Amelia County, site of Virginia's last major Civil War battle. Only seventy-two hours after their loss here, Confederate forces surrendered at Appomattox Courthouse.

Right: Assateague Lighthouse rises 142 feet above its island. Its beacon first beamed in 1867, and an automated light was installed in 1965.

Facing page: Mount Rogers Recreation Area in southwestern Virginia offers camping, cross-country skiing, horseback riding, and sixty miles of the Appalachian Trail.

A mystical sunrise in Shenandoah National Park.

Right: A Rockbridge County black oak tree, transformed by an ice storm.

Facing page: University Chapel stands near The Lawn and its buildings designed by Thomas Jefferson on the University of Virginia campus.

Above: Windpower in Williamsburg.

Facing page: Pastoral scene near Marion in Smyth County.

Sully Plantation in Fairfax County.

Charles Gurche is one of the United States' foremost nature photographers. His work has appeared in numerous magazines, including *Audubon*, *National Geographic*, *Natural History*, and *Outside*, and in the books *Missouri Simply Beautiful* and *Virginia Simply Beautiful*. As sole photographer, he has completed 70 calendars and six books, and has photographed for Kodak, the Sierra Club, Smithsonian Books, and the National Park Service. Awards have been presented to him by the Roger Tory Peterson Institute and the Society of Professional Journalists.